Original title:
Lilies of the Valley

Copyright © 2025 Creative Arts Management OÜ
All rights reserved.

Author: Rory Fitzgerald
ISBN HARDBACK: 978-1-80566-790-2
ISBN PAPERBACK: 978-1-80566-810-7

The Story of Beneath the Boughs

In the garden, blooms do wait,
A flower quiz with a twist of fate.
"I'm a tiny bell," they shrink and sigh,
"But my nickname's Ding-a-ling, oh my!"

Beneath the shade where secrets swell,
Critters gather for a gossip spell.
"Which plant's the tallest?" a squirrel grins,
"My acorn hat says, let the fun begin!"

Petals prance with petals bright,
Dancing in the morning light.
"I'll wear a crown while you go bare,
A funky flower, see me flair!"

A buzzing bee joins in the game,
"With my pollen basket, I'm never lame!"
"Join the fiesta, make some noise,
We're the wackiest garden joys!"

And so they play beneath the trees,
Creating chaos with such ease.
Nature's laughter fills the air,
With silly blooms beyond compare.

The Graceful Sway of Nature's Breath

In the garden where giggles bloom,
Bees in bow ties buzz with zoom.
Petals dressed in morning's cheer,
Dancing softly, drawing near.

With a wink, the breeze may tease,
Leaves do a jig, if you please.
Rooted jokes that never tire,
Whispers light as sparks of fire.

Journey Through Tender Vistas

Strolling paths of laughter's thread,
Tiny hats on blooms, it's said.
Nature's jesters, all outshone,
Crack a smile when they're alone.

Chasing shadows with a twist,
Every bloom a comical list.
Winking daisies, giggling soon,
Underneath the chuckling moon.

Portrait of a Quiet Spring

A canvas splashed with pastel glee,
Frogs in tuxedos croak with spree.
Petal pranks in playful light,
Whirlwinds of joy take flight.

Cuddly clouds drift hand in hand,
While sunbeam buddies make a stand.
Nature's quirks brushed with a smile,
Painting laughter all the while.

Beneath the Arched Canopy

Under wraps of green brigade,
Squirrels play charades in shade.
Tickling buds with a nudge,
Nature whispers, "Don't you judge!"

In this house of leafy fun,
Even shadows dare to run.
With every rustle, laughter springs,
A ticklish breeze that joyfully sings.

Conversations of the Untamed Heart

In a garden where giggles bloom,
Flowers chat in colorful loom.
"Hey, did you hear a bee's wild joke?"
"No, but I saw a snail who stoked!"

Bouncing bugs with a funny strut,
Dance and laugh in a big green hut.
"Why do you sway?" one petal asks,
"To keep the sun from wearing masks!"

Guardians of the Woodland

In the woods where whispers play,
Squirrels plot a nutty way.
"What's that sound? A branch that bends?"
"No, it's just the frogs—so many friends!"

Mice in armor, knights of cheese,
Plotting battles with triumphant ease.
"Have you seen the badger's dance?"
"Yeah, he's got a prancing chance!"

Basking in Nature's Ease

Underneath a sunlit tree,
Bumblebees sip their sweet tea.
"What's the buzz about today?"
"We're planning a floral ballet!"

Grasshoppers in a rhythmic leap,
Sing about secrets they keep.
"Why hop when you can glide?"
"Because I'm too short—can't hide!"

Ephemeral Moments of Joy

Petals laugh in a gentle breeze,
Whispering tales like giggly seas.
"Did you catch the worm's grand slip?"
"Yes, and I spilled my morning sip!"

Rabbits chuckle, tails a-flick,
Jumping over bushes—oh so quick!
"What's the best joke you've heard?"
"That one about the singing bird!"

Harmony in the Underbrush

In the thicket where munching bugs chime,
The plants gossip in rhythmic rhyme.
Frogs leap high in a silly dance,
While ants hold a parade by chance.

A squirrel steals a berry, what a show!
As dancing leaves put on a glow.
Rabbits giggle at the wiggly ants,
Nature joins in, wearing funny pants.

Blooms that Breathe with the Wind

Oh, how they sway, those flowers bright,
Bowing low to the breeze's light.
They gossip 'bout bees buzzing near,
And tickle each other, laughing dear.

Petals flutter like curtains in play,
As whims of the wind lead them astray.
A butterfly trips, what a sight to see,
For even in bloom, they find humor, whee!

The Silent Serenade of Nature

In a hush, the forest strums its song,
With a heartbeat that pulses along.
Beetles waltz with a twist and a twirl,
As shadows chuckle, they gladly swirl.

Mice share jokes with the wise old trees,
While shadows echo, 'Oh, do you please?'
Nature hums its silent parade,
Creating laughter that will never fade.

Twilight's Whispering Scent

As the sun sets, the fragrance draws near,
A scent so sweet, it brings a cheer.
Fireflies flicker like tiny stars,
In laughter, they'll dance without any bars.

The breeze carries whispers of secrets untold,
While flowers gossip of stories old.
A raccoon chimes in, tossing his hat,
In twilight's embrace, they all have a chat.

Petals of Hope in a Quiet Glade

In a glade where whispers play,
Tiny blooms joke all day.
They dance with bees in sunny cheer,
Validating each busy sphere.

Come and sip the nectar sweet,
Where tiny blossoms dance on feet.
They giggle as they sway and twirl,
A floral party, bright and whirled.

A Journey through the Fairy's Lair.

Through a tunnel made of light,
Fairies hover, oh what a sight!
Their antics cause the leaves to shake,
With every move, the mushrooms quake.

One pretends to be a frog,
Hopping 'round a squishy bog.
The others laugh, they can't control,
As a toadstool becomes their goal.

Whispers of the Forest Floor

Underneath where shadows fall,
Mossy beds hold voices small.
They chat of weather, bugs, and spouts,
And who has the best sit-and-pouts.

A squirrel joins with such a flair,
Wants to know if it's fair,
That mushrooms never seem to frown,
While he's stuck in nutty gown.

Beneath the Canopy's Embrace

In a canopy so wide and green,
A tapestry of sights unseen.
Giggling streams and flying leaves,
Share secrets that the daylight weaves.

A hedgehog shows off his new hat,
Made from petals, imagine that!
A parade of whimsy, cheer on high,
With nature's laugh beneath the sky.

Nature's Tender Elegy

In the garden, trees do sway,
Tiny bells dance in play.
Now a bug rolls by in style,
Wearing stripes, it flashes a smile.

Flowers giggle, they can't stop,
While clumsy ants all plop and flop.
A snail scolds with charming glee,
'Catch me if you can!' he teases the bee.

A Hidden Bower Awaits

Beneath the shade, a picnic spreads,
With sandwiches and dreams on beds.
A squirrel nabs a slice of cheese,
And shares it with the buzzing bees.

Butterflies play tag, they soar,
While daydreams tumble to the floor.
Leaves whisper jokes, their laughter bright,
As shadows dance into the night.

Reverie Amidst the Thicket

In the thicket, shadows tease,
A skipping frog, the crowd does tease.
He jumps and trips right on a stone,
Then croaks a tune that could be blown.

Bumbles buzz and twirl with zest,
Finding their way to a flower's fest.
A ladybug joins the fun parade,
Winking, she shows her little braid.

Charmed by Nature's Touch

The sun gives hugs to every sprout,
While clouds jump in for a playful shout.
A whiff of breeze, it spins around,
As nature's giggles fill the ground.

Tiny beings in a serve and spin,
A dance-off that surely must begin.
With petals fluttering in delight,
Nature's party lasts all night!

The Color of Serene Hues

In a garden full of cheer,
Bright blooms seem to appear.
They giggle when bees stumble,
As they trip and tumble.

With petals soft and white,
They dance in morning light.
Whispers of sweet perfume,
Fill the air with a boom!

Petal-Strewn Paths of Discovery

On paths lined with soft grace,
I skip with a silly face.
Chasing butterflies in flight,
I bump into a shrub, what a sight!

Every twist, a new jest,
Flowers playing hide and quest.
They chuckle as I fall,
Into greenery, I call!

Shimmers in a Deeper Green

In the forest's vibrant hue,
Where the green is bright and true.
The leaves try to wave hello,
But I trip over a toe!

Bouncing off each gentle stem,
Feeling like a little gem.
They giggle under the sun,
Guessing when I'll have fun!

Graceful Shadows and Light

In shadows where the light plays,
Flowers prance in their own ways.
They snicker at my brave stance,
As I try to join their dance!

The day ends with a twist,
A flower whispers, 'Don't resist!'
So I twirl with all my might,
And we laugh into the night!

The Fragility of Morning's Breath

A morning cup slipped from my grip,
The cat gave chase, a little trip.
Across the kitchen with laughter's chase,
I find my coffee in a silly place.

Butterflies dance in a hasty swirl,
I tried to catch one, gave it a twirl.
With socks on my feet, I dashed and spun,
Lost my balance, forgot how to run.

Serenity at the Edge of the Glen

A frog wore a crown, thought he was a prince,
He croaked out tunes that made me wince.
Songs of the swamp in a regal flair,
But all I could do was stand and stare.

A squirrel with shades, sipping his tea,
Mocking my dance, 'Come join the spree!'
I tripped on a twig, fell flat on my face,
He chattered and laughed, 'This is my place!'

Secrets of the Whispering Woods

The trees held secrets, but so did I,
My pants were stuck on a branch, oh my!
Whispers of leaves said, 'Get yourself free,'
While critters crowded, laughing at me.

A raccoon in spectacles, reading a book,
He looked over his glasses with a curious look.
I waved and I stumbled, misjudged my aim,
'Excuse me,' he scoffed, 'This isn't a game!'

Tranquility in the Silent Glade

In a glade full of flowers, I skipped with glee,
Tripped on a root, fell flat by a tree.
The blooms giggled softly, a mischievous sound,
As I rolled in the grass, feeling dizzy, unwound.

A bear in a tutu, what a strange view,
He spun in circles, as though he just knew.
Together we tumbled, a comical pair,
Nature's own ballet, with laughter in the air.

Tapestry of Graceful Leaves

In the garden, whispers play,
Dancing petals, bright and gay.
They giggle when the breezes tease,
Turning shy behind the trees.

With a twirl and a little spin,
They hide their laughter, a cheeky grin.
Golden rays, their favorite show,
As they chase the sunbeam's glow.

Every footstep sounds like beats,
A raucous symphony, oh so sweet.
Baking sun, they burn like toast,
But laughter always makes them boast.

At dusk, they settle with a sigh,
And share their secrets, oh so sly.
In the moonlight, they still prance,
In this midnight, lively dance.

Gentle Spirits of the Woods

In the woods where whispers roam,
Frolic figures call it home.
With twinkling eyes and winks so sly,
They trade their jokes with every sigh.

The mushrooms giggle, full of cheer,
As branches sway, we know they're near.
What tricks and tales will they confide?
A secret world, where they reside.

A snail once wore a fancy hat,
While squirrels chased a bouncing cat.
They roll in dirt and laugh with glee,
As laughter echoes merrily.

When sunlight fades, they bid farewell,
Yet dreams of mischief still compel.
Tomorrow's fun will start anew,
In the woods of magic, always true.

Petals Cradled in Green

Amongst the sprigs, a game unfolds,
Petals dressed in bright marigold.
They dare the dew to make them slip,
Laughing hard, they start to trip.

In playful prances, they spin and sway,
Chasing clouds that float away.
With nature's brush, they paint the day,
In colors that giggle, run, and play.

Bumbles buzz like tiny cars,
As ladybugs tell hilarious tales of stars.
A picnic feast of pollen and jam,
With ants in line, a marching band.

When evening falls, they nod and grin,
At the shenanigans, where do we begin?
With dreams of joy, they close their eyes,
In cozy green, beneath the skies.

Awakening of the Woodland Heart

As dawn breaks with a playful tune,
The woodland spirits wake up soon.
With stretch and yawn, they rise with flair,
Tickling ferns and tasty air.

A chipmunk pipes a silly song,
While wise old owls hum along.
The bushes sway, they jig and jive,
It's such a party, feel alive!

The sun peeks in with a nosey glance,
As flowers gather for a dance.
The roots below do tap their feet,
And every breeze hums to the beat.

At twilight's hush, they share a laugh,
As shadows paint the forest path.
With dreams so wild, they'll drift away,
And wake again for another play.

Delicate Blooms at Twilight

In the garden, tipsy sprites,
Dance beneath the fading lights.
Flowers chuckle, petals sway,
As critters join the night ballet.

A bee tells jokes, buzzing around,
While frogs in tuxedos leap and bound.
With every hop, a giggles bloom,
Creating a frolicsome, fragrant room.

Shaded Songs of Spring

Underneath the leafy roofs,
Worms do polka, share their goofs.
A robin croons a silly tune,
While raccoons join with spoons and moon.

Beneath a bush, a squirrel jests,
Wearing acorns as his vests.
Nature giggles in the sun,
A quirky party—oh, such fun!

Crystalline Petals in the Mist

Droplets sparkle, mischief's game,
As daisies plot to stake their claim.
A spider spins a web of glee,
While laughter wafts from every tree.

Marshmallows float on breezy dreams,
With butterflies in tea-time schemes.
The dawn breaks questions, here and there,
With fluffy clouds that tease and stare.

Fragile Treasures of the Glade

In shady nooks, the fairies play,
With twinkling eyes and wishes gay.
Toadstools laugh, embracing night,
Their caps aglow with mischief's light.

Old oak trees whisper tales of glee,
As dandelions blow, wild and free.
The glade is filled with joy, no doubt,
Where every step brings laughter out.

Secrets of the Open Glen

In a meadow bright with blooms,
A squirrel cracks its nutty dooms.
The flowers giggle with delight,
While bees are buzzing day and night.

A deer in specs plays chess all day,
While butterflies join the ballet.
The sun winks down with a smirk,
As rabbits plot their next great perk.

Grasshoppers dance to a tune unheard,
Some claim it's from an ancient bird.
They leap and hop in silly pride,
As nature rolls its eyes and sighed.

What secrets lie beneath the green?
A world of whimsy, bold and keen.
In every petal, every blade,
Lies laughter waiting to cascade.

Harmony Among the Moss

Among the stones, a lizard sings,
In harmony with frogs and flings.
The mushrooms nod with tiny grins,
As ants march forth with tiny bins.

A snail breaks dance, moves quite slow,
While crickets chirp in rhythmic flow.
The moss claims victory with its fluff,
And says, "You've never had it rough!"

In shades of green, a party grows,
Where every creature freely shows.
The toads are kings, the worms, their kin,
All share a laugh, and joy begins.

The sun peeks shy, its rays a tease,
While all the critters dance with ease.
In this damp world of friendly brawls,
The laughter echoes, nature calls.

The Aroma of Hidden Gardens

In gardens where the scents collide,
The gnomes hold meetings, side by side.
They argue scents, the good, the bad,
While roses giggle, all so glad.

A dandelion dons a hat so fine,
Declares to bees, "I'm a star divine!"
The daisies chuckle at the joke,
While bunnies join with hop and poke.

Thyme and mint play peek-a-boo,
Funny smells may ensue, who knew?
In a hidden nook, the herbs play charades,
While petals flutter in dance parades.

The scent of laughter fills the air,
As critters plot without a care.
In this garden, fun will thrive,
Where silly aromas come alive.

Softness in the Stillness

In corners soft where whispers play,
A sleepy cat naps the day away.
With yawns so wide and paws so round,
It's the fluffiest prince of the ground.

A hedgehog rolls in dreamland bliss,
While dreaming of a tender kiss.
The sleeping ferns sway to and fro,
As gentle breezes start to blow.

The quiet rustle tells a tale,
Of timid hearts that start to sail.
With every sigh, the day slips by,
Where every creature dreams to fly.

Yet in the stillness, jokes unfold,
As daisies whisper tales of old.
And in the shadows, laughter peeps,
Where softness in the stillness sleeps.

Dance of the Soft-Bellied Butterflies

In the garden, they twirl with grace,
Softly bouncing, a funny race.
Whispers giggle through the blooms,
Tickling petals, summoning looms.

With plump bellies, they glide and spin,
Chasing shadows with cheerful din.
Laughing leaves join in the spree,
Winking at bees in a reverie.

They sip nectar like gummy bears,
Flopping about, forgetting cares.
Who knew nature had a sense of play,
In a butterfly ballet, bright as day?

Red and blue, in sync they sway,
Bold performances, come what may.
Nature's jesters, alive and spry,
On blooming stages, soaring high.

Winter's Thaw and Spring's Revival

The snowmen attempted a dance,
But melted quick—what a mischance!
They slipped and flopped on puddled ground,
As sunshine's giggle spread around.

The icicles went for a dive,
Into the creek, oh what a jive!
A splatter, a splash, a frozen cheer,
As winter bids springtime to appear.

With blossoms sneezing, pollen flies,
Bunnies hop under sunny skies.
Worms shimmied up from their deep disco,
Spring's revival, nature's funny show!

Frogs croak out a zany tune,
While daisies wiggle beneath the moon.
This seasonal party brings delight,
As winter's slippers dance into the night.

The Lullaby of the Forest's Heart

In the forest, trees cozy and tall,
Squirrels chatter, having a ball.
Foliage whispers a silly song,
As the raccoons dance along.

Mossy beds become dreamy chairs,
Where owls hoot like they don't have cares.
The fireflies flicker like stars on cue,
Winking at shadows, playing too.

Branches sway, in a rhythmic swing,
Nature's lullaby, a giggling thing.
Woodland critters wear party hats,
Swaying along with the forest's chats.

When night falls, the fun won't fade,
Moonbeams laugh, soft beams cascade.
A lullaby of misfit dreams,
In the heart of the woods, humor beams.

Twilight Reveries in Pale Shades

Twilight paints the world so bright,
Shadows dance, a comical sight.
Bunnies prance in polka-dot clothes,
While crickets play their evening pros.

The sky giggles in hues of pink,
As fireflies wink, giving a blink.
Mice throwing a party, oh so neat,
Tiny sandwiches, a feast to greet.

Grassy carpets host silly games,
With laughter echoing lovely names.
The stars chuckle, twinkling above,
As twilight sings of nature's love.

Caught in reveries, a whimsical sight,
Where every creature's heart takes flight.
In pale shades, the world's a jest,
As night wraps all in a cozy rest.

Hidden Gems of the Green

In a nook where shadows dance,
Little buddies find their chance.
Wearing hats of chlorophyll,
They giggle, waiting for the thrill.

Puppy paws dig in the dirt,
A treasure hunt—oh, what a flirt!
Tiny bells on woodland stalks,
Whisper secrets to the foxes' talks.

Beneath the sun, they twist and sway,
In a game of hide-and-seek all day.
Who knew a patch could bring such glee?
Nature's laughs echo, wild and free!

Floppy leaves in a light breeze,
Cuddling daisies with such ease.
Peeking out, they're shy but bold,
These hidden gems—a sight to behold!

The Language of Soft Blooms

Whispers float on a gentle breeze,
Soft blooms share their secrets with ease.
"Bring the cake!" they seem to say,
With frosting laughs that brighten the day.

Dancing lightly, they jest and tease,
Waving hello with a shimmy and squeeze.
Pollinators stop for a tasty chat,
In a world where flowers wear a hat.

Swaying with laughter, they plot and plan,
"Let's throw a party!"—oh, what a clan!
Buzzing bees in a tuning fork chorus,
Filling the air with sweet giggles before us.

Through petals bright, adventures unfold,
In a garden where cheer is bold.
They write the script of the sun's delight,
With a chorus of blooms, they ignite the night!

Enchanted Raindrops on Petals

Raindrops tumble like joyful sprites,
Dancing on petals, they join the sights.
"Catch me if you can!" they gleefully shout,
Making puddles where giggles spout.

As the sun peeks, they start to twirl,
Each drop reflects a dreamy swirl.
"Can you hear us?" they chuckle in fun,
Waking up flowers, one by one.

Hopscotch on leaves, a splashy spree,
Shiny jewels, oh, how they agree!
Nature's charm in every drip,
With funny faces on each little sip.

A symphony of laughter unfolds,
With merry raindrops, a story told.
In the light of day, they caper and play,
Painting the world in a sparkling way!

Grace Beneath the Trees

Underneath where branches sway,
Squirrels chatter, birds on display.
Nature's stage with comic grace,
A leafy tap dance, the cutest face.

Laughter echoes, a soft refrain,
While shadows play their silly game.
"Look at that bug! It thinks it flies!"
The wise owls hoot and roll their eyes.

Rustling leaves hide giggly scenes,
Where woodland critters wear their jeans.
From tiny acorns, dreams take flight,
In a wacky world, full of delight.

As day turns night, the fun survives,
Moonlit antics to energize.
Beneath the trees, life's jest goes on,
With cozy whispers 'til the dawn.

The Embrace of Fragile Blooms

In a garden where whispers grow,
A dance of petals, soft and low.
They gossip with bees, oh such a tease,
Wearing white hats like they're at high tea.

With sunbeams tickling their tiny toes,
They sway along, where the light breeze blows.
Oh, clumsy critters, with legs so stout,
Trip on the blooms, let laughter shout!

A bumbling bug, in a fancy hat,
Dances with joy, then lands with a splat!
Yet petals don't fuss, they giggle instead,
Mischief and mirth, in the green bedspread.

So let's toast to blooms, fragile and bright,
That spread such laughter, a lovely sight.
With jokes in their leaves and jests in their roots,
They're nature's own clowns, in party suits!

Meadow Mysteries Unfolding

In a meadow where secrets hide,
Tiny sprites play, they take a ride.
On dandelion fluff, they soar and glide,
Making the flowers giggle and chide.

A deer with a wink breaks out in a trot,
Afraid of the giggles, but giving it a shot.
The cows in the field roll their eyes with glee,
As the chuckles spread like confetti, whee!

"What's that?" says the rabbit, peeking to see,
A snail making jokes, oh such jubilee!
His punchlines are slow, but clever and slick,
Leaving the audience laughing, oh what a trick!

So come join the fun in this meadow of cheer,
Where the whispers of nature bring laughter so near.
With secrets unfolding and smiles on display,
It's the funniest show, come out and play!

Lullabies of the Underbrush

In the underbrush, where shadows nap,
Creatures hold a soft, sweet laugh trap.
A squirrel on a branch, with nuts galore,
Drops one on his buddy, who's laughing (for sure!).

A hedgehog sings tunes, all poked and proud,
Filling the night with a giggly crowd.
While fireflies twinkle with sparkling light,
Winking at owls who are sleeping tonight.

"Oh hush," mumbles owl, with a voice so deep,
"Can't you keep it down? I'm trying to sleep!"
But the critters just chuckle, with glee in their hearts,
As laughter and lullabies play their parts.

So rest in the underbrush, dreams take flight,
With funny tales weaving through the night.
For in this wild concert of nature's embrace,
Every creature shares a warm, laughing space!

The Memory of Softness

Softness whispers like a breeze in May,
Bringing smiles to all, brightening the day.
A fluffy cloud floats, oh, what a hoot,
Tickling the flowers with a light-hearted toot.

A rabbit hops in, with a twitch of his nose,
Tickled by petals, like tickling toes.
"What's your secret?" he asks, with a giggle,
"To be so soft, it makes me wiggle!"

Then comes a turtle, slow but wise,
Chiming in gently, "It's all in the size!
Small hearts can giggle, and softness is grand,
Just look at my shell, it gets a laugh band!"

So cherish the softness, in smiles we find,
Memories blossom, and laughter is kind.
In a world of whimsy, just open your eyes,
Softness and humor make the sweetest ties!

Beneath Nature's Gentle Tapestry

In the woods where whispers play,
Little flowers hide all day.
Dancing bees with tiny feet,
Say, 'Come join our floral feat!'

Grasshoppers leap, with silly flair,
Tickling toes in the fresh air.
Squirrels giggle, chasing leaves,
While cheeky crows steal from thieves.

A hedgehog wears a tiny crown,
His spikes a jolly, prickly gown.
So many critters look and stare,
At blooms that giggle, unaware.

Nature crafts this bright parade,
Each bloom a joke that won't fade.
With laughter sprinkled all around,
Joy in petals can be found.

Serenading the Awakening Earth

A bunny hops with floppy ears,
Tickling petals, spreading cheers.
The sun peeks through the leafy shroud,
As laughter echoes soft and loud.

Beetles sing their funny tune,
Bouncing like a merry balloon.
With every step, a giggle bursts,
In nature's choir, joy must thirst!

The daisies wink at passing ants,
Wearing hats like fancy pants.
Each blossom holds a sly little jest,
Creating smiles, we feel blessed.

As morning wakes and yawns its way,
Nature's humor saves the day.
A jokester blooms, just take a glance,
In this grand, whimsical dance.

The Essence of Shy Blooms

Hidden blooms in secret corners,
Whisper jokes to passing mourners.
With shy delight, they peek and smile,
Throwing charm in playful style.

A timid bud starts to quiver,
As butterflies begin to shiver.
"Guess my color!" it dares to sing,
While crickets join, doing their thing.

A snail slides up, slow and grand,
With a message from the land.
"Why rush? Life's a little tease,
Let's chill and dance among the trees!"

Nature's humor, sweet and sly,
Mixes giggles with the sky.
Underneath the gentle light,
Funny blooms bring sheer delight.

Nature's Heartbeat Underfoot

Padded steps on a leafy ground,
Hidden laughter all around.
Each footfall taps a quirky beat,
Echoing joy that can't be beat.

Caterpillars in funny hats,
Wobble by with chirpy chats.
While mushrooms giggle in delight,
Inviting all to stay for a bite.

Roots chuckle beneath the soil,
Sharing secrets with gentle toil.
A playful breeze whispers through,
Jokes of nature, old and new.

With every step, a hearty tease,
Flowers dance in the warming breeze.
Where laughter grows, the heart takes flight,
In nature's wonder, pure delight.

Secret Grace of the Woodland

In secret glades where laughter swells,
A tiny bell sings sweet farewells.
With milky white and cheeky grins,
They play hide and seek, like true old friends.

In leafy hats, they strut about,
With whispers soft, they twist and shout.
Nature's jesters in a fray,
Who knew blooms could be this gay?

Their porcelain cups hold nectar bright,
Sipping sunshine, a pure delight.
With every breeze, a giggle clear,
The woodland elves just can't endear.

So next you roam through dappled shade,
Look closer for the jokes they've laid.
These little blooms, like jesters bold,
Hide secrets plenty, and stories untold.

Echoes of Dappled Sunlight

In sunlight's dance, the shadows play,
With petal hats upon their sway.
They grin at bees that buzz and bumble,
With each soft sway, their fun's a jumble.

A squirrel stops, a curious glance,
As flowers twirl in summery dance.
Their whispers tickle a summer's breeze,
Causing chuckles among the trees.

"Join us here!" they seem to shout,
As butterflies swirl, roundabout.
The dance goes on, a lively show,
Nature's comedy in vibrant glow.

With cheeky smiles, they nod in mirth,
In this joyous, sunny earth.
So come and laugh with blooms so bright,
In echoes of this sheer delight.

A Dance of Fragility

With delicate steps, they sway and bend,
In the woodland's air, they twist and send.
A ballet light, a subtle tease,
Whispers laughter through the leaves with ease.

They tease the breeze with gentle sways,
In a playful game of hide and stays.
While fungi chuckle at their show,
In the softest spots where wild laughs grow.

With petals soft, they steal the scene,
In nature's theater, where all convene.
Fragile yet fierce, they shine and play,
Turning the ordinary into a ballet.

So tiptoe near this giggling crowd,
Among the blooms, so free and proud.
These light-footed friends brought joy to all,
In the dance of fragility, they stand tall.

Morning Dew's Gentle Caress

As dawn awakens with a yawn,
The drops of dew come, fresh and drawn.
Kissing petals with gleeful glee,
"Look at us!" they giggle with glee.

They puddle up like tiny pearls,
Every bloom dons new twinkling swirls.
A morning hug, soft as a sigh,
Whispers secrets as the clouds drift by.

"Oh don't you dare," they seem to chant,
"For the sun will melt us into slant."
In giggles shared as light creeps in,
The day begins, let the fun begin!

So splash through morn, where giggles reign,
Among the dew and petal planes.
With every drop, a chuckle found,
In morning's light, pure joy abounds.

Veiled Elegance of the Earth

Beneath the green, they wobble and sway,
With whispers of charm, come out to play.
Dressed in white, so cute and spry,
They giggle in gardens, oh my, oh my!

They fool the bees with their tiny shows,
Dancing so fast, yet nobody knows.
A game of peek-a-boo in the grass,
Invisible flowers, how long will they last?

With coats of dew and sunshine's steal,
They tiptoe around, an amusing reel.
Eavesdropping on gossip from the blooms,
As petals plot their secret costumes.

So here's to the blooms, with laughter and jest,
In this green stage, they're truly the best.
With each little sway and each little grin,
The earth's own jesters, let the fun begin!

Where Shadows Meet Light

In the dusk, they're sneaky and sly,
Peeking from corners, where strange critters fly.
Catching the sunlight, in a playful bind,
Their jokes are secret, you'll only find.

One whispered to me, just the other day,
'Why do we bloom? Just to keep gray away!'
With a wink and a nod, they giggled aloud,
'This life is pure joy, we're far from the crowd!'

They frolic in shadows with a daring dance,
Inviting the whimsy into their prance.
With every twirl and with each little shake,
They remind us to laugh, for happiness' sake.

So embrace all the tricks that nature invents,
With petals for curtains, and humorous hints.
In the garden of light, where shadows may glide,
Let's toast to their joy, with laughter as our guide!

Breath of Innocent Flora

Tiny white hats that bob in the breeze,
Whispering secrets to curious bees.
They wear such charm, with innocent flair,
Stirring up giggles with scents in the air.

One little bloom said, 'I'm quite the catch,
I'll make all the bunnies stop, look and scratch!'
With laughter and cheer, they pave their way,
A chorus of jokes in the light of the day.

Squeezing through soil, they plot and conspire,
To turn up the green, and spark their own fire.
Imagining worlds where they reign supreme,
Adventurous sprites in a mischievous dream.

So let's dance with the flora, with giggles in tow,
For laughter is endless in their playful glow.
With each little breeze, bring joy to the plot,
For in every giggle, you'll find a sweet thought.

Moonlit Winding Trails

Under moonlight, they sway and they twist,
A jolly parade that you simply can't miss.
With each little step on this winding spree,
They whisper sweet jokes, just for you and me.

Wobbling with laughter, they join the night's cheer,
'Why be a wallflower, when the moon's here?'
In shadows they teeter, in light they stand tall,
The world is their stage, oh, they have a ball!

With petals that giggle and leaves that hum,
They spin little tales till the morning comes.
A festival of joy, dressed up in gray,
They'll dance till the dawn, come what may.

So heed their soft chuckles, their bright merry trails,
For life is a party when laughter prevails.
With the moon as their spotlight, in a grand ballet,
Let's waltz through the night in a whimsical way!

A Tapestry of Innocence

Amidst the leaves, they peek and play,
Little bells giggle, bright and gay.
A game of hide and seek they hold,
With whispers sweet, their stories told.

In frocks of white, they dance around,
On softest mounds, without a sound.
Their laughter echoes through the air,
A secret choir, beyond compare.

They tease the bees, oh what a scene!
Dancing petals in the green.
With every breeze, a ticklish sigh,
Who knew plants could be so spry?

A tapestry woven, laughter bright,
Nature's jesters, pure delight.
In innocence, they sway and flower,
Tickling hearts within the bower.

In the Arms of the Verdant Whisper

In emerald realms where whispers bloom,
Tiny pals escape the gloom.
With every giggle, the leaves shake,
Nature's own delight, no mistake.

Oh, watch them wiggle, watch them sway,
In a leafy cabaret, what a display!
With petals soft, they flip and flop,
A froggy leap, and then they hop.

Stirring up trouble with every cheer,
Inviting a squirrel to join near.
Together they twirl in the sunny ray,
Making mischief in their play.

In the arms of the whispering trees,
They frolic and dance on the breeze.
What a jest, what a splendid spree,
In nature's heart, they're wild and free.

The Unseen Beauty of the Crescent

In shadows hushed, they wink and blink,
A crescent smile, pause, and think.
Unseen blossoms in playful tease,
With laughter tangled in the breeze.

Oh, silly sprites in evening's glow,
Casting spells, stealing the show.
With moonlit dreams that twirl and sway,
They beckon night to join their play.

A candid chuckle from the gloom,
As stars peek in to check their room.
The unseen beauties take their flight,
Chasing shadows into the night.

In the mystery of twilight's grace,
They sprinkle laughter, life, and space.
With every giggle, glowing bright,
Nature's jest fills the starry night.

Gentle Hues in Nature's Cloak

In tones of green, they come alive,
Jolly little caps, what a drive!
In the forest, they host a feast,
Bringing chuckles, to say the least.

Ticklish leaves brush against their cheeks,
In such folly, the nature speaks.
With every swirl and playful dive,
A giggly buzz where fun can thrive.

They bounce in rhythm, side by side,
With sprightly glee, they turn the tide.
Painting the ground with laughter's brush,
In nature's cloak, a joyful hush.

Gentle hues, in playful chase,
Crafting joy in its own embrace.
Nature's jesters, bright and bold,
Sewing true magic, laughter retold.

Portrait of the Verdant Veil

In a forest bright and merry,
A flower danced, oh so airy,
With petals wide and colors bold,
It winked at bees, quite uncontrolled.

A squirrel passed, with twitching tail,
He tripped on roots, began to flail,
The flower chuckled, having fun,
Nature's prank was just begun!

From sunlight's beam, a shadow leapt,
A rabbit plotting, quietly crept,
He thought he'd sneak a taste so sweet,
But ended up with muddy feet!

The merry blooms will always cheer,
With laughter ringing, far and near,
In every petal, a giggle hides,
While nature plays, the frolic abides.

Twinkling Stars Among the Foliage

In twilight's grasp, the stars peeped out,
The leaves below began to shout,
'Look up, look up!' they rustled loud,
As fireflies formed a twinkling crowd.

A clumsy owl took flight by night,
But tangled up in branches tight,
The stars all giggled, bright and bold,
While he went turning green and cold!

A raccoon laughed, tipping his hat,
'You're quite the scene, oh silly bat!'
And all the critters gathered 'round,
To watch the owl and laugh profoundly.

The moon looked down with knowing smiles,
'Nature's stage gets funnier by miles!'
And in this forest, so alive,
Laughter echoes, as they thrive.

The Elixir of Nature's Breath

In a meadow, lush and grand,
A rogue breeze swept across the land,
It tickled flowers, ran amok,
And startled each snug little rock.

A dandelion began to sway,
It burst out laughing, bright and gay,
While ladybugs in spots of red,
Joined in the chorus, merrily led!

A butterfly with painted wings,
Danced through petals, spun like kings,
A thistle frowned, all spiked and gruff,
'Why can't we all just chill and fluff?'

With every gust, the giggles grew,
As wind played tricks on critters too,
Nature's laugh, a soothing balm,
In this vast world, it feels so calm.

Soft Whispers in the Wilds

In the woods where whispers blend,
A tree swayed, its branches bend,
It sneezed a cloud of pollen wide,
Of course, a nearby beetle cried!

A patch of grass began to sway,
'Excuse me, leaf, you're in the way!'
And all around, a gentle tease,
As nature danced with playful ease.

A spider spun a web so bright,
It gleamed and shone with morning light,
But caught a bug, who squealed, 'Oh no!'
'This isn't quite the show I know!'

Yet through the giggles and the glee,
Nature thrives, forever free,
With every whisper, soft and light,
The wilds keep chuckling through the night.

Sweet Surrender of the Evening Dew

The dew drops dance on leaves so green,
Like tiny jewels, they shimmer and preen.
The critters giggle, a slippery sight,
As they slip and slide in the soft moonlight.

A snail slides by, with a grace so rare,
Claiming he's quick, in the cool night air.
"You'll never catch me!" he boasts with glee,
While mice just chuckle, sipping their tea.

The breeze plays tricks, it teases the grass,
Making them sway, as if they were class.
A rabbit hops, thinking he's so sly,
But stumbles on clover, oh my, oh my!

So here's to the night, full of laughter bright,
Where even the bugs have silly delight.
With dew on their heads, they dance around,
In this funny kingdom, joy can be found.

The Hidden Gem of the Grove

In the quiet grove, old trees take a bow,
Beneath their shade, the critters know how.
A squirrel pretends he's a grand old queen,
As he struts with nuts, so proud and so keen.

Frogs hold a band with croaks and loud croons,
They jam in the night, beneath glowing moons.
The fireflies flicker like tiny bright stars,
They twirl through the air, ignoring their scars.

A hedgehog tiptoes, trying to blend,
But rolls to the side, and now he must fend.
"I'm just practicing!" he shouts in reply,
While the others just snicker and roll on the sly.

So raise up a toast to this jolly old place,
Where laughter and fun put a smile on each face.
Among ancient oaks and the roots like a maze,
Life's quirkiness sparkles, a jovial haze.

Petals in the Shadow's Caress

In shadows deep, where mischief breeds,
Petals plot out their floral misdeeds.
A dandelion whispers, with a cheeky wink,
"Bet you can't catch me – I vanish, I stink!"

The daisies join in, playing tag with the breeze,
"Catch us if you can! We'll bend at the knees."
A bumblebee buzzes, so round and so fuzzy,
Crashing in flowers, feeling all dizzy.

Petals unite, a colorful crew,
In a petal parade, just for a few.
A butterfly flips, but stumbles in glee,
"Do they really think they can out-fly me?"

So in the soft shadows, where humor collides,
Life's silly moments like a funny ride.
With petals and laughter, each giggle and cheer,
They bloom in the night, spreading joy far and near.

Echoes of Pastels in the Mist

The morning mist hides mischief in dream,
Where petals tease petals, or so it would seem.
A tulip trips over a dainty old vine,
"Watch where you're going; you crossed the wrong line!"

A pastel parade, with colors so bright,
Each flower dances with all of their might.
A shy little rose hides behind a bush,
But the daisies pull jokes, creating a rush.

"Who's the fairest?" they'd laugh in their bloom,
As violets jive to dispel any gloom.
With petals giggling, and bees making plans,
They toss out their pollen like confetti in fans.

So join in the fun, in the soft morning light,
Where laughter and petals make everything right.
In echoes of pastels, mischief persists,
In a garden of humor, it's never amiss.

The Hidden Heart of Spring

In the garden where gossip blooms,
Daisies tease the tulips' plumes.
A bee with dreams of nectar sweet,
Tripped on petals, oh what a feat!

The sun's a joker, spreads delight,
While clouds play hide and seek in flight.
A squirrel on a flower chair,
Claims royalty in his fluffy hair!

The scent of mischief fills the day,
As blooms conspire in their own way.
With whispered jokes in winds so light,
Spring's laughter echoes, pure and bright!

Whispers in the Verdant Grove

In the grove where secrets play,
Leaves giggle, come what may.
A rabbit dons a stylish hat,
While birds compose a chirpy chat!

Mice wear shoes of tiny size,
Stomping through the petals' prize.
An orchestra of frogs does croak,
Underneath the golden oak.

Butterflies with polka dots,
Dance around in funny spots.
As the silly blooms just sway,
Spring's laughter leads the way!

Serene Adventures in Petal Land

In Petal Land, the smiles grow,
With flowers that twirl in a show.
A snail wore shades to shield its eyes,
From petals throwin' surprise skies!

Ants march like they own the place,
Each carrying crumbs at a brisk pace.
A ladybug ran a stumble race,
Fall in love with the lovely space!

The sun beams down with a wink,
While flowers giggle and think,
Chasing dreams where laughter rings,
In this realm where joy takes wings!

A Soft Glimpse of Timelessness

In the dusk, petals twirl and sway,
Colors mingle, evening's play.
A hedgehog dons a fancier guise,
With daisies laced in mismatched ties.

The twilight whispers, laughter rings,
As crickets tune their tiny strings.
While a clever fox tells a tale,
Of dance-prone blooms and a ship's sail.

With stars peeking through the gloom,
Moths hold a ball, find their room.
In this soft glow, fun unfurls,
A timeless dance in petal twirls!

Timid Blossoms in the Dawn

In morning light, they shyly peek,
With tiny bells that softly squeak.
Dancing 'round, a little shy,
They giggle as the sun goes high.

Petals whisper, 'Catch us fast!'
As breezes tease their fragile cast.
A game of hide, a playful race,
Against the wind, they find their place.

A Symphony of Soft White Chimes

Beneath the trees, they sway and swing,
A chorus built for laughs to ring.
With every gust, a jolly sound,
As mischief in the air is found.

Chiming bells in sunlight's glow,
Playing tricks, oh what a show!
Catch a friend in laughter's snare,
As petals wink without a care.

Murmurs of the Shaded Path

In secret shades, the gossip flies,
As flowers share their silly sighs.
"Did you hear?" one blooms will say,
"Last night, I danced the night away!"

Old roots chuckle, bending low,
While young buds twirl with grandiose flow.
A pathway lined with giggles bright,
As petals flutter in delight.

Beneath the Boughs of Serenity

Here under branches, all looks grand,
With tiny sprites that laugh and stand.
Whispers drift like smoke in air,
Inviting smiles, no room for care.

Bouncy blooms, they tease and play,
In their dim nook, bright thoughts display.
"Who needs a crown?" one flower beams,
"When petals float, it's just like dreams!"

The Gentle Call of Wildness

In the garden, whispers tease,
Where tiny blooms sway with ease.
They giggle and sway in afternoon light,
Dancing with bugs, quite the sight!

A squirrel stops, does a little twist,
While blooms stick out their tiny fists.
"You're silly!" they chime with delight,
As butterflies join the wild flight!

With petals dressed in bright array,
They prank the ants who march and play.
"Catch us if you can," they shout,
In the wild, there's never a drought!

Just watch the chaos unfold so grand,
As greenery joins the jolly band.
In this patch of riotous cheer,
Nature's own comedy is near!

A Symphony of Hidden Flora

Among the leaves, a melody hums,
Tiny blossoms playing their drums.
A chorus of colors, so bold and spry,
Making merry while butterflies fly!

"What a tune!" yells a bumblebee,
As blooms nod along in harmony.
With a jig and a wiggle, they steal the show,
While the sunbeams giggle, putting on a glow!

Each petal has dreams of becoming a star,
Yet all they do is sit, not go far.
"Let's throw a party!" a daisy cries loud,
As violets blush, hidden in a crowd!

A tinkle of laughter, a rustle of leaves,
They sway to the rhythm while the gardener grieves.
For every time he tries to prune tight,
They play hide and seek, sneaky and light!

The Realm Where Petals Dance

In a realm where the petals all twirl and spin,
A pint-sized party is sure to begin.
The daisies wear hats made of finest grass,
While tulips in skirts take turns to prance!

"Watch my moves!" cries a bold sunflower,
As the breeze gives them quite the power.
With giggles and twirls, they step to the beat,
Even a snail joins, quite light on its feet!

The giggling buds take off on a spree,
A hop and a skip, so wild and carefree!
While bees breakdance, on nectar they feast,
In this cheerful lawn, no joy is in least!

The grass sings along with a rustling cheer,
As frogs jump in, croaking loud for the beer.
In this dance of flora, where silliness reigns,
Every leaf finds a friend, and laughter remains!

Nature's Sweetest Lullaby

When the moon peeks out, the flowers hum soft,
In their secret caverns, they begin to loft.
They tell bedtime tales to the ants and the moon,
With lullabies drifting like a sweet tune.

The sleepy petals yawn and fluff,
"Tomorrow we'll dance, isn't that enough?"
While the stars twinkle, play their own game,
The flowers settle down, never looking the same.

A gentle breeze weaves stories anew,
About a bold bee who fancied the dew.
With humor and charm, they drift off to dreams,
Where flowers wear jeans and burst at the seams!

So close your eyes tight and dance in your sleep,
Join in the fun where secrets run deep.
In this garden of giggles, relax and abide,
As the petals sway gently, on laughter they ride!